Gardening with Mommy

Includes many fun and educational gardening activities for children and their families to enjoy all year round.

Gardening with Mommy book Published by:
Straight Forward Technologies
www.straightforwardtech.com
Roger & Kristen Joyal
P.O. Box 102, Valley Center, KS 67147
Phone: 316.207.3211
Email: info@gardeningwithmommy.com
Website: www.gardeningwithmommy.com

"The love of gardening is a seed that once sown never dies"
Gertrude Jekyll

Table of Contents

Table of Contents

Table of Contents

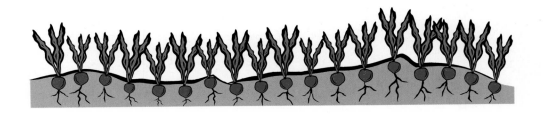

"Let's Get Ready To Garden"

Introduction

From the time I was a young girl growing up in Anthony, Kansas, right in the heartland of the United States, I can remember the joy I felt planting the first flowers and seeds in the cool spring soil.

I have fond memories of the large gardens that I planted, weeded and harvested with my parents, and how wonderful it felt when our harvest was so abundant that it overflowed the kitchen. Whether it was planting flower seeds in the flowerbeds or growing corn and tomatoes amidst my dad's wheat, my love for gardening has flourished over the years.

Now that I am raising my own children I enjoy sharing my love for gardening with them. This book is a combination of gardening projects that I enjoyed while I was growing up, with new creations that I have tried with my own children.

I believe that *how* we spend time with our children when they are young is as important as how *much* time we spend with them. What time could be better spent than sharing the joys of gardening.

"Mothers plant the seeds of love that bloom forever"

Beyond the Clouds,
Beyond the Rain,
There are a Thousand Rainbows.

Chapter 1

Theme Gardens

Wizard of Oz Garden

Being from Kansas, this garden was a very special one for us to design. You can decide what elements you want to include, as there are many options. I recommend watching the *Wizard of Oz* before starting to design your garden. The movie gave us such inspiration before we even started to design the garden.

Scarecrow

Your *Wizard of Oz* Garden will not be complete without a scarecrow. You can design your own or use the materials and plans provided. To construct, nail the pieces of wood in a "T" shape to make the arms. Dress and then stuff your scarecrow with the plastic trash bags. Paint the facial features on the flowerpot and allow to dry. To attach head, place plastic washers on top of the pot and screw into the top of the wood stake, being careful not to over tighten. Attach hair and hat with hot glue.

Yellow Brick Road.

Stepping stones, corn, poppies and other red plants are added.

Materials:

2 Pieces of 2" x 1" Wood
  (1 longer than the other)
Nails (to connect wood)
Flower Pot
Long Screw with Nut
Plastic Washers
Raffia for Hair
Hat
Child-Size Clothes
Paint for Face
Trash Bags
  (to stuff scarecrow)

Three friends gather in the garden.

Tin Man Windchime

I found the plans for this tin man at www.hobbylobby.com. The kids just loved making it, but it does require a lot of adult help and supervision. If you don't have the exact size of cans the plans call for, you can always substitute another similar size can.

Materials:

Ice Pick
Clothes Hanger
Wire Cutters
2 - 1" Wood Screws
2 - 1" Moveable Eyes
32 oz. Coffee Can
13 oz. Coffee Can
2 - Sardine Cans

1 - 1/2" Metal Screw with Nut
20 oz. Fruit Pie Filling Can
4 - 15 3/4 oz. Vegetable Cans
Acrylic Paint - Black, Red
Silver Spray Paint
6" Funnel
4 Soft Drink Cans

Instructions: Go to www.hobbylobby.com, click on crafting ideas and then search for tin man. Here you will find the complete assembly instructions.

Materials:

Round Stepping Stone   **Spray Adhesive**
Yellow Concrete Paint   **Red Glitter**
Child's Dress Shoes   **EnviroTex Lite™ Pour-On**
Red Spray Paint   **High Gloss Finish**

Ruby Slippers

These beautiful slippers are easy and fun to make. Spray paint a pair of shoes red and let dry. Spray the shoes with a spray adhesive glue and sprinkle red glitter until the shoes are covered. To adhere the shoes to the yellow stepping stone, place them on stepping stone and then pour the high gloss finish over the shoes and stone completely covering both. Let dry completely before placing outside in your garden. Follow the manufacturers directions when preparing the finish.

There Is No Place Like Home

Grow a Pizzeria Garden

What is your favorite food? If pizza is at the top of your family's list, then this is one garden for the family to plant. You can grow everything you need to make your own pizza sauce and some pizza toppings. Kids love this garden because it actually takes on the shape of a pizza!

1. Purchase concrete edging to make the "pizza crust." The garden shown here used 24 pieces of concrete edging.

2. Cut 8 foot landscape timbers to slice your pizza into segments.

3. Plant the "pizza garden" plants in different segments of the pizza. Onions and Garlic can be planted together and Basil, Oregano and Marjoram can be planted in the same segment. Place plant markers next to each type of plant.

Plants:

Tomato Plants
Bell Pepper Plant
Banana Pepper Plant
Basil Plant
Oregano Plant
Marjoram Plant
Garlic Cloves
Pineapple Plant
Onion Sets

Materials:

Brown Concrete Edging
8ft. Landscape Timbers
Red Mulch for Sauce

4. Finally, add a little "pizza sauce" to your new garden with some red colored mulch. Watch your garden grow and enjoy your pizza all year long!

Homegrown Pizza Sauce Recipe

Ingredients:

4 large tomatoes, skinned and chopped
¼ C. chopped onion
2 T. chopped garlic
1 T. chopped fresh basil
1 t. chopped fresh oregano
1 t. chopped fresh marjoram
¼ t. pepper
2 T. olive oil

Directions:

Remove the skin from each tomato by placing it in boiling water for approximately 15 seconds. Remove from the boiling water and place in cold water to stop the cooking process. When cool, remove the skin and core.

To make the sauce: Heat olive oil in a saucepan over medium heat. Sauté onions until tender. Stir in garlic, and cook for 1 minute. Crush tomatoes into saucepan. Add basil, oregano, marjoram and pepper. Simmer for 10 minutes.

The "Wild" Animal

Plants:

Hen & Chicks
Tiger Lily
Lamb's Ear
Elephant's Ear
Zebra Grass
Leopards Bane
Pony Tail Grass
Leopard Marigolds
Monkey Grass
Crocodile Snapdragon
White Swan Echinacea

1. Determine the shape and location of your garden. We decided to plant our "Wild Animal Zoo Garden" in a leopard shaped bed, although most would say it looked more like our cat. You can shape your garden any way you wish, as a zoo animal or just in your normal flower bed. Spray paint can be used to outline the shape of the garden, and then the grass can be removed.

2. Fill the garden with your favorite plants that have zoo animal names. Most plant nurseries will have their inventory on a computer system and will be able to do a search for various plant names.

3. If you have any zoo animal figurines or garden statues, these can also be placed throughout the garden. Plant name markers in the shape of the zoo animal can also be added to complement the garden theme.

Zoo Garden

Zoo Garden Inspiration

This is a garden that all animal lovers will go "wild" over.   A trip to your local zoo can provide great inspiration as you look for plants that are named after all your favorite zoo animals.   Take a pad and pencil with you so your kids can write down the names of animals. If your local plant nursery has a plant catalog you can take that along with you as well.

Easy to Grow Herb Garden

Herbs are so much fun to grow. You can start most of the "kitchen" herbs indoors in the winter if you want, or wait and buy the plants in the spring. You can use fresh herbs in dishes you are preparing, and also dry the herbs for use all year around. Whatever you decide to do with the herbs, children can easily grow them.

Plants:

Basil
Chives
Oregano
Parsley
Thyme
Coriander

Beautiful blooms adorn these chives when not being harvested.

Fresh parsley garnishes grilled chicken at a summer BBQ.

Early in the spring, the herb plants had already started to fill in this small flowerbed.

Spaghetti Sauce Garden

1. Prepare the garden area by tilling the soil and adding compost. You may want to use landscape timbers to section off the garden.

2. Add the tomato sauce plants listed below. The size of your garden area will determine how many of each plant you will need.

3. To add the final tomato sauce look to your garden, add red mulch around your plants. You may also want to place a plant marker next to each plant.

Spaghetti Sauce Recipe

4 C. chopped tomato
¼ C. diced onion
¼ C. diced pepper
½ t. basil
½ t. oregano
½ t. thyme
½ t. fresh parsley
1 clove garlic—minced
¼ t. salt
¼ t. black pepper
2 T. olive oil
2 T. brown sugar

Sauté the onion, pepper and garlic in the olive oil for several minutes. Add the remaining ingredients and simmer for 30 minutes. Serve over cooked spaghetti squash or pasta.

Plants:

Tomato
Onion Sets
Bell Pepper
Basil

Oregano
Thyme
Parsley
Garlic
Spaghetti Squash

Plants:

Chocolate Beauty Sweet Pepper
Chocolate Lace Foamy Bells
Mint Chocolate Foamflower
Chocolate Veil Coral Bells
Chocolate Mint Geranium
Chocolate Birthday Cake Foamy Bells
Chocolate Mint
Chocolate Ruffles Coral Bells
Chocolate Cosmos
Chocolate Caricature Plant
Chocolate Chip Bugleweed
Chocolate Soldier Columbine
Chocolate Boneset
Chocolate Vine
Chocolate Plant

Mulch:

Hershey™ Cocoa Bean Mulch

Plant Markers:

If your family likes to paint, preparing plant markers for this garden will be a great family activity. All you need is some thin pieces of wood and stakes. Ours were painted brown (like chocolate) with white writing. If you are really creative, you may want to make a sign that looks like a candy bar and says "Chocolate Garden."

Hershey's™ Cocoa Bean mulch was the inspiration for this garden. I have always loved the wonderful smell the mulch gives throughout the yard. Surprisingly, you can also find a large number of plants that have chocolate in their name. Many plant nurseries have computer systems that can search plant names for key words. Even better, many of these are perennials, so you can enjoy them year after year.

18

Grow An  And A

Materials:

Garden Space
Swan Gourd Seeds
Apple Gourd Seeds

I had never grown gourds as a child, but when I saw these seed packets I just couldn't resist. The swan gourd plant produced a large gourd with a slender, arching neck. Children and adults alike will enjoy painting or making a birdhouse out of it. The apple gourd looks like a giant apple that is just perfect to decorate for your favorite teacher.

1. After the danger of frost is over and the soil temperature is 65 degrees, prepare a space to grow your gourd garden.

2. To help with germination, lightly nick the seed coat of each seed. The seed producer recommends not cutting too deeply and staying away from the seed tip. Soak the seeds in room temperature water for 24 hours before planting.

3. At the end of summer when the vine is dry, pick the gourds and allow them to dry in an airy warm location. Drying is complete when the seeds rattle inside.

19

Rainbow Garden

"Somewhere over the rainbow"...... this wonderful, colorful garden can be planted in the shape of a rainbow. Don't forget to add the finishing touch, a pot painted gold and filled with yellow trailing flowers.

Materials:

Annual Bedding Plants
   Orange
   Yellow
   Red
   Blue
   Purple
   Green
Pot Shaped Planter
Gold Spray Paint
Potting Soil for Planter

1. After the danger of frost is over, head to your local plant nursery to check out the selection of colorful annuals.

2. Some colorful annuals that are easy to find are marigolds for the orange and yellow colors in the rainbow, salvia for the red, petunias for the purple and blue hues and then look for a plant with pretty green foliage.

3. The pot we used in our garden was originally a black plastic planter. We used gold spray paint to give it the shiny gold appearance. For drainage, drill a few holes in the bottom, add pea gravel and then fill with a good potting soil. We filled the pot of gold with yellow petunias that would eventually trail over the side.

Just a Note:

Unfortunately, we never saw this garden grow to maturity and therefore do not have any other pictures. The entire garden died in one day after spray that was intended to kill weeds in the yard apparently drifted into the rainbow garden.

This is the Rainbow Garden just after being planted.

The Itsy Bitsy Spider

Materials:

Old Rubber Tire
8 - ½ Inch (inside diameter)
  Self Sealing Rubber Pipe
  Insulation Tubes
2 - Plastic Softballs
Black Paint
Drill - 1 ½ inch Hole Saw

Plants:

Cobweb Hen & Chicks
Red Cloud Spiderwort
Sweet Kate Spiderwort
Spider Plant

1. Once you have found an old tire, purchased the flexible insulation tubes and located Dad's drill with a bit that will cut holes in the tire, you are ready to create this unusual garden.

2. Drill 4 holes on each side of the tire. These will hold the 8 legs of the spider. Only drill holes through the top sidewall.

Climbed Up The Water Spout

3. Determine where you are going to grow your Itsy Bitsy Spider Garden and place the tire in the desired location. Insert each spider leg into a hole in the tire. Bury one foot of the other end in the dirt. Continue until all of the spider legs are in place.

4. Fill the tire with dirt, packing it around each leg. Plant the Cobweb Hen & Chicks, one or two varieties of Spiderwort, and a spider plant. The Cobweb Hen & Chicks is one of my favorite plants and was the inspiration for this garden. Although many people are familiar with Hen & Chicks, this variety actually looks like it has cobwebs on it. Everyone you know will definitely love this plant.

5. The finishing touch on this garden will be the "spider eyes." Using two hollow plastic softballs, mask off half of the ball and spray paint the other half black. This black portion will be the back of the eye. Paint a black circle in the middle of the other white half to create the eyeball.

6. Drill two holes in the front of the tire. Use clear Liquid Nails™ glue to attach the eyes. Masking tape may be needed to hold the eyes in place until the glue is dry.

7. If desired, create a spider web garden sign to place behind your spider.

★ Outerspace Garden ★

Plants:

Flying Saucers Coreopsis
Blue Moon Lobelia
Ruby Moon Hyacinth Bean
Rocket Mix Snapdragon
Arctic Star Geranium
Atlanta Moonlight Daylily
Sterling Star Verbena

Stardust Mix Impatients
Moon & Stars Watermelon
Saturn Sun Coleus
Cosmic Yellow Cosmos
Falling Stars Vine
Sky Flower
Moon Glow Hosta

This garden will be a favorite for boys and girls to plant. Our family really worked together to design the flying saucer and the space man scarecrow. You will probably have just as much fun explaining to your neighbors about your unique garden. Plant markers can be helpful as you share your garden with others. We grow so many different types of plants that I have a hard time remembering every plant's name. The mulch in this garden is white marble "Moon" rock.

Space Man Scarecrow

Materials:

*2 Pieces of 2" x 1" Wood
(1 longer than the other)
Nails (to connect wood)
Spacesuit Costume
Black Gloves
Plastic American Flag
Plastic Trash Bags
Plastic Fish Bowl
American Flag Sticker
White Krylon™ Spray Paint
Black Acrylic Paint
Paint Brush
Masking Tape
Newspaper Scraps
1—1 inch Screw
Plastic Washer*

Space Man Scarecrow

What would an outer space garden be without a space man. This patriotic scarecrow is bound to delight all who come to visit your garden.

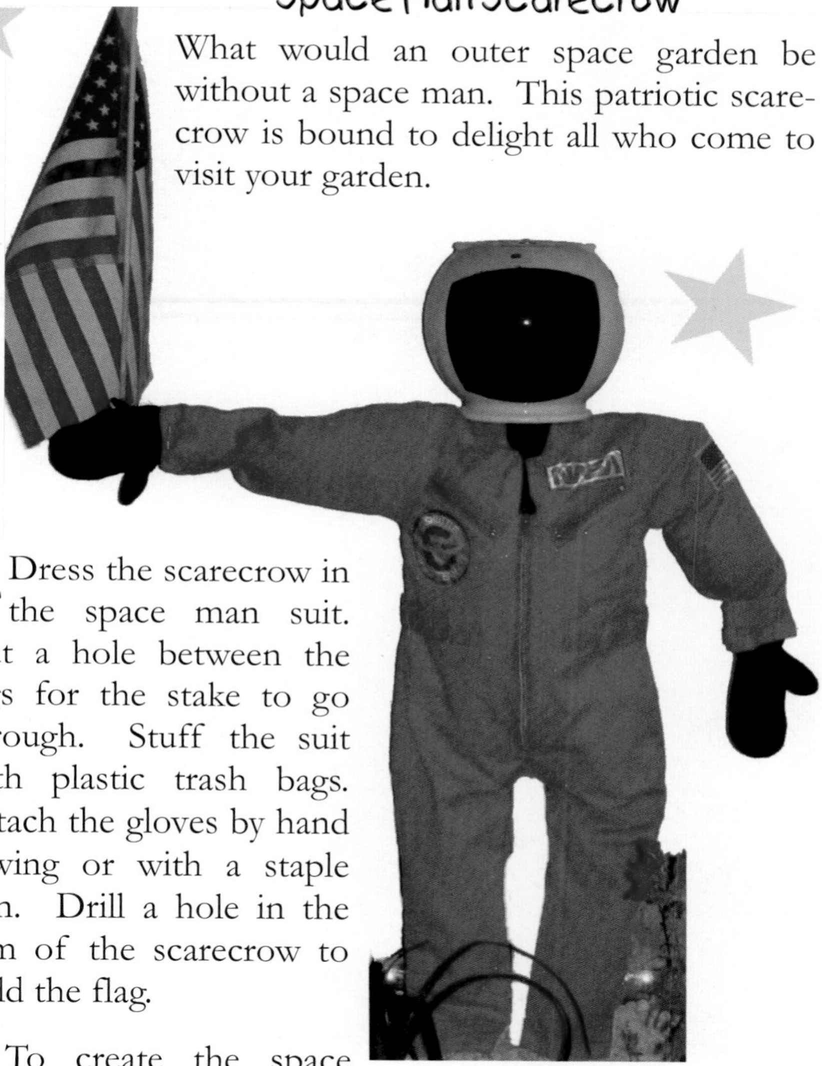

1. Prepare the frame of the space man by cutting one piece of wood the length of the space suit with an extra foot added to stake into the ground and extra for the depth of the fish bowl. Cut an additional piece of wood to use as arms. The length of the arms will vary depending on whether you want both arms out straight or one arm down as shown here. A screw and washer will be used to attach the top of the fish bowl to the wood.

2. Dress the scarecrow in the space man suit. Cut a hole between the legs for the stake to go through. Stuff the suit with plastic trash bags. Attach the gloves by hand sewing or with a staple gun. Drill a hole in the arm of the scarecrow to hold the flag.

3. To create the space helmet, the inside of a clear plastic fish bowl was painted with white and black paint. Tape off and cover the area that will be black with masking tape and newspaper. Use Krylon™ Fusion spray paint to paint the white area.

After the tape and newspaper are removed, the black face mask area can be painted with a brush. Add an American Flag sticker for a finishing touch. Attach the helmet and place the space man in your space garden.

Flying Saucer

This flying saucer found the perfect spot to land in the Outer Space garden. Made with two inexpensive saucer sleds, a plastic bowl and rope lights, it certainly made an interesting addition to the Outer Space garden.

Materials:

2 Saucer Sleds
1 String Clear Rope Lights
Clear Liquid Nails™
1 Plastic Bowl

6- ¼ Inch Screws
Silver Krylon™
  Fusion Spray Paint
Black Paint
3—12 inch Bolts
6—Nuts

1. Paint the outside of each sled with Krylon™ Fusion paint.

2. Drill three holes for the bolts (landing legs) in one of the saucers. Thread a nut onto each of the bolts. Insert the remaining threads through the saucer holes, then thread on a second nut onto each bolt. The saucer will be sandwiched between the nuts.

3. To attach the sleds together, place a thin bead of liquid nails around the outside edge of each sled.

4. Place the glued edges of the sleds together and then place screws around the edge for extra stability.

5. To provide the finishing touch, use clear glue to attach the plastic bowl on top and the rope lights around the edge pf the flying saucer. Paint windows with black paint. Bury the bold head 3 to 4 inches deep.

Hawaiian Aloha Garden

Aloha! You will definitely want to welcome this HOT garden to your landscape. Complete with a volcano, lava rock and fun fiery plants, family members of all ages will enjoy building, planting and, finally, watching this garden EXPLODE at the end of the season.

Materials:

Plastic Megaphone Cone
1 bag Quikcrete™
Water
Shovel
1 liter bottle (empty)
Brown Spray Paint
Red Acrylic Paint
Lava Rock

Plants:

Pineapple Plant
Molten Lava Coleus
Explosive Blast
Ornamental Pepper
Hawaii Blue Ageratum
Ananas Lucidus Red Pineapple
Volcano Coleus
Sizzler Red Salvia

1. After preparing the Hawaiian Aloha Garden site, place the cone shaped megaphone over a plastic 1 liter bottle. The bottle will be used to hold lava mixture when the volcano erupts later in the season.

2. Pour one bag of Quikcrete™ into a wheelbarrow or large bucket. Add water according to the directions and stir with a shovel.

3. Cover the top of the cone with masking tape on the bottle cap to keep water and bugs out until you are ready to explode the volcano. Mold and form the concrete around the cone, making a volcano shape. Use a pointed object to make lava flow indentions down the volcano.

4. Use brown and red paint to add the final volcanic touch to your explosive volcano.

5. Plant a variety of the Hawaiian and volcanic named plants, mulch with lava rock, and wait for your garden to grow.

Explosive Blast Recipe

You know what they say, an erupting volcano is sure to draw attention and a crowd. That is what happened when we erupted our volcano. All the neighborhood kids gathered to share in the excitement. We waited until the end of the growing season, just in case the plants didn't appreciate the vinegar, baking soda and dishwashing soap. We were lucky, though, and all the plants survived the "eruption."

Ingredients:

1 Cup Water
1 Cup Vinegar
1 Tablespoon Liquid Dishwashing Soap
2 Tablespoons Baking Soda
Red Food Coloring
1 Square Sheet of Toilet Paper

Directions:

Pour the water, vinegar and food coloring into the plastic bottle. Place the baking soda in the middle of the sheet of toilet paper and fold in edges to make a pouch. Place the pouch into the bottle, move away and wait for the ERUPTION!!!

Note: The volcano can be erupted more than one time. To keep water and leaves out of the bottle, just cover it with tape once the bottle is dry.

ABC Garden

Materials:

Garden Space
2"x4"x8' Wood
Saw
Paint
Popsicle Sticks
Staple Gun
Flowers from A to Z

My daughter Ashlyn was just getting ready to start Kindergarten when we planted this garden in the flowerbed around her playhouse. What fun we had looking through all the plants at the stores for certain letters of the alphabet. If you have perennials already growing in your yard, take a cutting of those first to help save on the cost. You can also check with neighbors or friends and see if they have any they can offer. Since we only needed one plant for each letter, we purchased packs of flowers for other areas in our yard and just used one of them in this garden.

The photograph above was taken in August. Some plants tried to overtake the others and had to be continually trimmed back. Notice the peach tree in the bottom right corner. It was started from seed only a year ago.

ABC Garden

ALPHABET PLANTS:

A
Aster, Alyssum

B
Begonia, Baby's Breath

C
Coleus, Cosmos

D
Daisy, Daylily

E
Elephants Ear

F
Foxglove, Fiber Optic Grass

G
Geranium

H
Heather, Hen & Chicks

J
Jacob's Coat

K
Kiss Me Over the Garden Gate,

L
Lamb's Ear, Lavender

M
Marigold, Moneywort

N
Nasturtium

O
Oregano, Onion

P
Pansy, Poppy, Phlox

Q
Queen Anne's Lace

R
Rosemary, Russian Sage

ALPHABET PLANTS:

S
Scented Geranium, Scardy Cat, Snapdragon

T
Thyme, Tiger Lily

U
Umbrella Plant, Universe Plant

V
Venus Fly Trap, Verbena, Vinca

W
White Sage, Wormwood, Wizard Pineapple Coleus

X
Xanthosoma (Elephant Ear)

Y
Yarrow, Yellow Poppy

Z
Zinnia, Zebra Grass

To create plant markers, cut the wood into 26, 4-inch pieces. Paint the wood a solid color. When dry, paint a letter of the alphabet on each piece. An easy way to stake the letter into the ground is to attach a popsicle stick to the back of each letter with a staple gun.

Gardening Rocks Garden

Materials:

Garden Site
Landscape Fabric
Landscaping Rock
Acrylic Craft Paint
Varnish
Paint Brushes
Rock Garden Plants

1. Prepare the garden site and cover the soil with landscaping fabric.

2. Determine where each plant will be placed and cut holes in the fabric. Plant the rock garden plants like Hen & Chicks and sedum.

3. Select smooth rocks to be painted. Wash, with soap and water and then allow to dry several days. After painting, apply a varnish coat to protect them from the elements. Once dry, add rocks to your garden and enjoy all year long.

Above is our rock garden before the kids added their painted rocks. Notice how much more alive the garden becomes with their unique, colorful rocks.

Candy Garden

Plants:

Candy Floss Blue Bacopa
Duet Candy Stripe Portulaca
Christmas Candy Coleus
Peppermint Candy Geranium
Elegant Candy Daylily
Strawberry Candy Daylily
Candy Stripe Phlox
Sugar Candy Clematis
Candy Corn Vine
Buttercup
Tutti Frutti Giant Hyssop
Double Bubble Mint Giant Hyssop
Lemon Licorice
Licorice Splash
Jelly Beans Stonecrop
Peppermint Mint
Strawberry Geranium
Chocolate Cosmos
Penny Candy Violet Bacopa
Buttered Popcorn Ranunculus
Chocolate Mint Geranium

What a sweet treat this garden will be to your landscape. Add personalized plant markers for a fun craft project.

Candy Corn Vine

Peppermint Candy Geranium

Penny Candy Violet

Christmas Candy Coleus

Buttered Popcorn

Chocolate Mint Geranium

Stop and look at the world through the eyes of a child.

Chapter 2

Salad
Garden

Container Gardens

Salad Container Garden

Materials:

Large Planter
Packing Peanuts
Potting Soil
Your choice of plants:
  Lettuce Varieties
  Broccoli
  Cauliflower
  Cucumber

Even if you don't have a garden area in your yard, you can still enjoy an early spring "salad garden." All you need is enough space for a planter, some warming sunlight and water. This container garden is great for the cool spring time when the ground is still warming up. If you get an unexpected frost, just bring your container garden inside for the night.

1. Put a layer of packing peanuts in the bottom of a large planter. This will help make the planter lighter and easier to move around.

2. Fill the planter with potting soil. Leave 2 to 3 inches at the top of the planter for mulch and watering.

3. Plant your favorite "salad" plants in the planter. Water on a regular basis and soon you will be enjoying your homegrown salad.

Gardening Note

The photograph on the previous page is what our salad garden looked like after only 5 weeks. We started harvesting broccoli about 9 days before this photograph was taken. Besides being really yummy and healthy, this garden was a beautiful sight in early spring.

Crock of Soup Garden

1. Check the planter to see if drainage holes are provided. If needed, drill five or six holes in the bottom of the pot and then add a layer of pea gravel to the bottom of the pot.

2. Fill the pot within two to three inches of the top with potting soil.

3. Sprinkle the seeds on the top of the soil. With your hand (or paw), stir the seeds gently into the soil. Cover lightly with additional soil if needed. Gently add water to your soup by sprinkling it with water, cover (with plastic wrap) and wait for the soup garden to grow.

Materials:

Plastic Pot Planter
Pea Gravel
Potting Soil
Soup Mix Collection of Beans
Plastic Wrap

I purchased the seeds for this garden at our local health food store. It had a soup mix collection in a self-serve bin. When I went to pay for the bean collection, I had to pay only twenty-five cents. Wow, what a deal!!!!

Sweet Potato Pie Garden

This is a great way to grow sweet potatoes if you are short of space or if you have heavy clay soil. What really made this garden so much fun to grow, was not knowing if it would work at all. Imagine how excited we were at the end of the summer when we discovered how many sweet potatoes were hidden inside our planter.

Materials:

Chicken Wire
Landscape Fabric
Pliers
Compost
Potting Soil
Sweet Potato Plants

1. Make a cylinder with the chicken wire. Use pliers to bend and secure the chicken wire at the seam.

2. Place landscape fabric around the inside of the chicken wire. Add compost and soil to hold the fabric in place.

3. Plant several plants in the top of the garden. Cut small holes in the sides of the garden and place plants in each hole, packing the soil around each plant. Water regularly.

This is what the potatoes looked like with the wire and fabric removed.

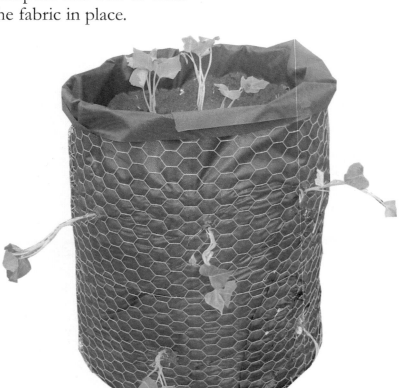

Alan and his mom show the sweet potato harvest.

Swimming Pool Garden

Materials:

Plastic Swimming Pool
Pea Gravel
Potting Soil
Plants and Seed

If you don't have abundant garden space, this garden is the perfect solution. Children absolutely love it when they can have a special garden that is all their own. As you prepare to plant your garden, plan a special trip to the store or local plant nursery to pick out the seeds and plants to add to their new garden.

1. To insure proper drainage in the swimming pool garden, drill drainage holes throughout the bottom of the swimming pool.

2. Find the spot where you want to grow your swimming pool garden. Add a layer of pea gravel to the bottom of the swimming pool. Fill within 2 inches of the top with a good quality potting soil.

3. Plant a variety of plants and seeds in the soil. Try to arrange the plants and seeds according to the height they will grow, with taller plants in the back. Remember to water regularly. Plants in pots and above ground containers dry out more quickly than plants in the ground.

Although we didn't follow the rules of necessary spacing between plants, the year we planted this garden, Ashlyn was able to harvest tomatoes, cucumbers, green beans, a watermelon and even a few ears of corn.

Peanut Butter & Jelly Garden

1. If you decide to use a container for this garden, you will need to provide good drainage. Make sure that there are drainage holes in the bottom of the container. If needed, drill several holes. Add a layer of gravel or packing peanuts in the bottom of the container.

2. Fill the container with a good quality potting soil. Leave 2 to 3 inches at the top to allow room for mulch and for watering.

3. Soak the peanuts, still inside the shell, overnight in a bowl of water. The next day, plant each peanut, with the shells attached, in the middle of the container 1 to 2 inches deep. Leave room to plant the strawberry plants around the outside of the container. Cover firmly with soil but do not pack the soil too much. Keep the soil moist, but not wet, until the peanuts sprout in one to two weeks.

4. Plant the strawberry plants around the outside of the planting container. Keep the entire garden watered. During the hot days of summer the container will need to be watered on a daily basis. Plants in containers will dry out faster than plants in the ground.

5. As the peanut plants grow you will notice yellow blossoms. These blossoms indicate that the plant is setting on peanuts. To decide when it is time to dig the peanuts, carefully dig up a peanut hull and check the color. If the hull is white it is not time to dig your peanuts. If the hull is dark then the peanuts are mature and ready to dig. Gently loosen the soil around the plant and shake off as much soil as possible. Allow the plants, with the peanut still attached, to dry for 2 to 4 weeks. If you have a place to do so, hanging the plants can be very

Materials:

Garden Space or
Large Whiskey Barrel
Potting Soil
Gravel or
Packing Peanuts
Peanut Seeds or
Raw Peanuts from the
Grocery Store
Strawberry Plants

helpful in curing the peanuts. After the peanuts are cured, take them off the plant and store them in a cool dry place.

Useful Information About Growing Peanuts

Whether you grow this theme garden in your vegetable garden or in a container, children and adults alike will have a great time watching peanuts grow.

The container garden will work great in areas with clay soil. By using the container you can grow the peanuts in a good quality potting soil.

Peanuts have a long growing season of 130 to 140 days, so you will need to plant them as soon as the threat of frost has passed, or start them indoors if you have a short growing season in your area.

When choosing strawberry plants, find a variety that bears fruit all summer. This way your family can enjoy the fruit continuously while you wait to harvest the peanuts.

Cactus Boot Garden

Materials:

6 Small Cactus Plants
Cactus Potting Soil
Sand or Gravel
Rocks
Old Pair of Adult Size
  Cowboy Boots

1. Fill the cowboy boots halfway full of sand or gravel for drainage.

2. Fill the remaining portion of the boot with potting soil specifically made for cactus plants. Leave 3 inches at the top for plants and rocks.

3. Plant the cactus plant in the soil at the top of the boots. Use tongs or gloves to help protect your hands from the cactus thorns. Add additional soil if needed.

4. Add rocks around each cactus plant and water lightly.

Cactus Growing Tips

Cactus plants are easy for children to grow inside the house. They love light, but not too much water. Water only occasionally, with lukewarm water, when the soil is dried out. Your cactus will thank you if you fertilize it once a month, using an all-purpose brand at half strength. With minimal care required, this unusual garden can save an old pair of boots and be an usual conversation piece in your home.

Colander Herb Garden

Your kitchen cabinet is as far as you need to go to find this plant container. If your family doesn't have an extra spaghetti colander, check your local dollar discount store.

Materials:

Colander
Potting Soil
3 to 4 plants

Possible Plants:

Tomato
Onion
Chives
Parsley
Basil
Marjoram
Pepper

1. Fill the colander ½ full of potting soil.

2. Position the plants in the colander.

3. Fill the colander within an inch of the top with the potting soil. Gently water your new garden.

Gardening Tip

Drainage will be a challenge with this cute kitchen garden. Make sure to water the garden daily. You can make cute plant markers by painting the names of the plants on wooden spoons and placing them in the soil.

Litter Box Garden

You will definitely please any kitty cats that are members of your family with this garden. Have you ever noticed that many cats like to chew on houseplants? Cats are naturally drawn to green plants, many of which are poisonous to them. So what could be better than to plant them some kitty cat grass that will provide them with vitamins and minerals that they need. To find the perfect seed blend for your cat, visit your local pet store, or do a search on the internet for cat grass seed.

Litter Box Garden

Materials:

Plastic Litter Box
Potting Soil
Cat Grass Seed Blend

1. Fill the litter box within one to two inches of the top with potting soil.

2. Sprinkle the soil with the cat grass seed. Lightly cover the seed with potting soil. Gently water the seed and keep moist until the seed sprouts in only a few days.

3. After the seed sprouts, move the garden into a sunny spot and lightly water on a daily basis. Be careful not to water too much though, as mold could start to grow.

4. When the cat grass is four or five inches tall it is ready to serve to your favorite kitty cat. The grass will last for a couple of weeks.

Our own family kittens Oakie Dokie and Kailey were happy to get the opportunity to satisfy their "green" tooth with this garden. Oakie tried to help us plant the seeds and was very curious about what we were planting in this litter box. If the litter box garden is too big for your cat family, plant a smaller amount of seed in another type of planter.

TOMATO HUMOR

Why did the tomato turn red?

Because he saw the salad dressing.

Chapter 3

Outdoor Gardening

Cotton Garden

While I was researching, growing and writing this book, I stopped by a cotton gin near my childhood hometown of Anthony, Kansas, one early spring day to see if I could get some cotton seeds. I had never grown cotton before, but I was always amazed when I saw those huge fields of cotton, white as snow in the fall. I just knew that my children would be fascinated as they watched this plant grow and the cotton develop.

The picture above, taken in October, shows a cotton field in southern Kansas.

When you see cotton flowers like the one above, you will know that cotton will soon grow on the plant.

This shows cotton in two different stages.

Materials:

Garden Area or Planter
Cotton Seed
Cotton Boll Compost
Cotton Boll Mulch
Potting Soil

1. Prepare the garden site. I love to work some cotton boll compost into all areas of my garden, although it is particularly fitting for this garden.

2. Plant seeds 6 to 12 inches apart and ½ inch deep.

3. Keep the ground moist until the seeds sprout.

4. After the plants are established and the ground temperature is warm, you can mulch with cotton boll mulch if it is available in your area.

5. Harvest cotton bolls in late fall for bouquets or crafts.

Cotton Seed Information

If you live in a rural area check your local Coop for cotton seed. If you need additional information about how to get cotton seed go to www.gardeningwithmommy.com. If you do not have outdoor garden space to grow this crop, consider growing cotton as a house plant.

Tree Blossom Bouquet

The first signs of spring often appear on our trees. If you have a tree that flowers in the spring, and that maybe needs a little pruning., you can trim off a few branches, place them in a vase, and bring a little spring indoors. Let the children help you arrange the blossom branches for a beautiful spring bouquet.

Materials:

Flower Vase
Tree Blossom Branches
Pruning Shears
Water

Trees that flower in the Spring

If you want to plant trees that will flower in the spring consider some of these varieties. To find the specific variety of tree that will grow contact a local plant nursery or extension office.

Flowering Pear
Purple Leaf Plum
Dogwood
Weeping Cherry
Magnolia
Peach
Redbud
Crabapple
Cherry

"The Earth laughs in flowers"

Ralph Waldo Emerson

49

Balloon Plant Garden

Adults and children alike will be absolutely amazed to watch fast sprouting radish seeds grow inside a clear balloon. After planting a balloon, be careful that it doesn't "pop," or you will have potting soil all over. After perfecting this activity, try sprouting different kinds of seeds to see which work the best.

Thanks to www.recipes4learning.com and www.gratefulkids.com for sharing this wonderful gardening idea. If you are wondering why the balloon doesn't deflate like a normal balloon, your family can research how plants create oxygen through the process of photosynthesis.

Balloon Plant Garden

Materials:

Clear Balloon
Potting Soil
Radish Seeds
Funnel
Water

1. Place the neck of the balloon around the funnel.

2. Spoon small amounts of potting soil into the funnel until the deflated balloon is full.

3. Add 10 to 15 radish seeds to the soil through the funnel.

4. Add water a teaspoon at a time until the deflated balloon is full.

5. Blow up the balloon and immediately tie it. Gently shake the balloon to help settle the potting soil, seed and water mixture.

6. Place the balloon in a sunny location and wait only 24 to 36 hours before the seeds begin to sprout.

7. After about a week the soil will start to dry out. The balloon can be carefully cut open and the plants transplanted.

Wheat Initials

This is a great fall, winter and spring activity. After planting the wheat seed in the fall, you will be able to watch your initials or name grow during the winter, and then grow tall and produce wheat in the spring and early summer. Plan to use your homegrown wheat in a creative way by making a wreath, a flower arrangement, or a wheat kernel picture.

1. To prepare the ground for planting, till and rake until the ground is very smooth.

2. Using a hoe, write your name or initials in the soil. Plant the wheat seeds in the soil where your initials are carved, placing seeds 1 inch a part. Cover with ½ inch of soil and gently water the seed. Keep the soil moist until the seeds sprout, and then water as needed.

3. Watch and wait until early spring, when the wheat will begin to grow. Depending on the area of the country where you live, the wheat will be mature in June or July.

Materials:

Garden Space
Wheat Seed

Note: There are some regions of the United States that plant a variety of wheat that is planted in the spring and harvested in the fall.

Fun Plants to Grow

Bananas

Who would have known that a banana plant would grow so well in Kansas. Our banana plant spent the summer outside and then was brought indoors before the first frost. Be aware, bananas require a lot of water. We are still waiting to see if it will ever set on bananas. If your local nursery does not have banana plants, they can be ordered on-line.

Pumpkins

If you have room in your garden, a pumpkin patch is fun for children to grow. There are so many different varieties available on the market, you will have a hard time deciding which one to plant. If you want to harvest pumpkins by Halloween, be sure to plant your seeds by the Fourth of July (at least that is the rule we follow in Kansas). When the pumpkins are small, children can carve their initials into the pumpkin and then watch it grow throughout the summer.

Tomatillos

The tomatillo originated in Mexico and is commonly used in many Mexican dishes. A member of the tomato family, the plant grows like a tomato, but the fruit has a husk that must be removed before eating. If you decide to grow some tomatillos in your own garden, find a recipe for "salsa verde" and share this Mexican recipe with your family.

53

Rules for a Child's Garden

1. Plant Smiles
2. Grow Giggles
3. Harvest Love

Chapter 4

Indoor Gardening Activities

Grass Sock Caterpillar

Materials:

Socks
Potting Soil
Grass Seed
Rubber Band or
Ponytail Holder
Materials for Eyes,
  Nose, Mouth & Bows

1. Pour some potting soil into a bowl.

2. Add some grass seed to the potting soil and mix them together.

3. Fill each sock with the potting soil and grass seed mixture.

Have you ever wondered what you could do with all those socks that somehow have lost their mate in the laundry? This caterpillar is the perfect solution. Find several socks of different sizes and colors to help you grow your caterpillar family. Colored socks will look better than white socks after growing for a couple of weeks.

4. Roll the open end of the sock up and secure with a rubber band or a ponytail holder.

5. Decorate your caterpillar with a bow to cover up the rubber band, and then add the eyes and nose. Let your own creativity be your guide.

6. Lightly spray or mist the outside of the caterpillar with water. Continue to water daily and soon your caterpillar will come alive with green.

Goldfish Plant Garden

When I saw the goldfish plant at a local store, the first thought that came to mind was the empty fish bowl in our basement. This plant has beautiful orange—red flowers that really do resemble goldfish. The blue colored sand added just the right watery touch and really helped bring out the color of the flowers.

1. Fill the fish bowl part way with potting soil.

2. Add the goldfish plant. Add more potting soil.

Materials:

Fish Bowl
Potting Soil
Colored Gravel or
*   Colored Sand*
Goldfish Plant

4. Place the fish bowl in a sunny location and water as needed.

3. Add a layer of colored gravel or sand to complete the fish bowl garden.

Crystal Rock Garden

The next time you are shopping for laundry detergent, be sure to throw some Mrs. Stewart's Bluing™ into your shopping cart as well. This easy project will yield amazing results for your family. To use as a science project, check out Mrs. Stewart's web-site for a scientific explanation.

Materials:

Old Pie Pan
¼ C. Mrs. Stewart's Bluing™
¼ C. Salt
¼ C. Water
1 T. Ammonia
Rocks
Small Pieces of Coal

1. Combine the bluing, salt, water and ammonia in a container. Stir to mix.

2. Place some small rocks and coal into an old pie pan. Slowly pour the bluing mixture over the rocks and coal. As the water evaporates, watch the crystals start to grow.

3. To add color to the garden, add drops of different colors of food coloring over the rocks and coal. To keep the crystals growing, add more of the mixture to the bottom of the pie pan.

Fun Plant Planters

Juice Box Planter

Coconut Planter

To use a coconut as a planter, have an adult use a power saw to cut a small hole in the top of the coconut. Clean out the inside of the coconut, fill with potting soil, and add a small houseplant.

Baby Bottle Plant Nursery

Add a little fun to your planting projects by looking for unusual planters. Kids love the juice box drinks available at the store. To use as a planter, cut the top off with scissors, pour the juice into a cup, and then wash the container with soap and water. Add potting soil and a favorite flower or herb and you have a fun, colorful planter. One extra bonus is that with the clear back, you can watch the roots of the plant grow.

Little girls will love using old baby bottles for plant nurseries. The baby bottle on the left was filled with root watering crystals and water. It is fun to watch the roots grow.

Rainbow Bouquet

This colorful experiment is one that will amaze children of all ages. After placing cut carnations in different colored water solutions, children can enjoy watching the color move up the stem to the petals.

Materials:

5 or more Cut White Carnations
Red, Yellow, Blue, Green, Purple & Orange
  Food Coloring
Water

A similar activity can be done by placing one end of a freshly cut celery stick in some colored water. After a day or so, what do you think will happen?

1. Fill each vase or glass with water and add enough food coloring tom make the water very bright.

2. Add the white carnations to the vases of colored water. Within 6 to 12 hours you will begin to see the color making its way into the veins of the carnations.

3. Once the carnations reach the desired color, cut ½ inch off each stem at an angle and place all the colored carnations in a vase for a beautiful presentation.

Layered Soil Dessert

This dessert is fun to make any time of the year. If you make one for each member of your family, place them on the table at each setting to help decorate the table while you eat your main course. The recipe makes one dessert, so plan accordingly if you are going to make more. For even more fun, purchase miniature garden trowels for your guests to "dig" into their soil dessert.

Ingredients:

8 Oreo™ Cookies
1 Ding Dong™ Cake
1 Chocolate Pudding
  Snack Size
Chocolate Whipped Cream
Gummy Worms
Flowers
Plastic Wrap
Clear Plastic Cup Size
Plastic Bag

1. Place the Oreo™ cookies into a large plastic Zip-Lock™ bag. Using a rolling pin, crush the cookies into fine pieces. Add ½ of the cookies to the bottom of the cup. Reserve the remaining cookie crumbs for later.

2. Chocolate pudding is the next layer in the soil dessert. Spoon one snack-size container of chocolate pudding over the Oreo™ cookie pieces.

3. Crumble one Ding Dong™ cake and sprinkle it over the pudding.

4. Put a couple of gummy worms on top of the pudding around the edge of the cup so they can be seen from the outside. Add the chocolate whipped cream for the next layer of the dessert.

5. Add more gummy worms over the whipped cream, and top with the remaining Oreo™ cookie crumbs.

6. Finally, add a stem or two of real or artificial flowers to your yummy soil creation. If you decide to use real flowers, it is recommended that you wrap the stem in plastic wrap before inserting it into the soil. Refrigerate until ready to serve.

Grocery Store Gardening

The next time you get the gardening bug in the middle of winter, head straight to your local grocery store to find some exotic and fun indoor plants. From your favorite citrus fruits to avocados, beans, pomegranates and even rice, your family will have a great time experimenting with these indoor gardening ideas.

Growing Papaya

Papaya is a fruit that not everyone has tried. You definitely should purchase one with the extra bonus that you can grow a very interesting houseplant from the seeds inside a papaya.

1. Cut the papaya fruit in half as shown in the picture below. Spoon the seeds into a strainer and rinse with water.

2. Place the seeds in a cup of water and allow to soak overnight. If any seeds float to the top, spoon them out and toss them in the trash.

3. Plant the seeds ¼ inch deep in a good quality potting soil. Cover the planter with plastic wrap until the seeds have sprouted. Water on a regular basis, keep the plant in a bright location, and fertilize occasionally.

From Seed to Houseplant

Plants you can grow from seed:

Grapefruit
Lemon
Orange
Lime
Avocado
Papaya
Peach
Sweet Potatoes
Beans
Pomegranates
Apple
Cherry
Potatoes

Avocado Plants

The best way I have found to grow an avocado plant is to plant the seed in potting soil with the pointed end up. Keep the soil moist and in a couple of weeks the seed will sprout. Place the plant in a sunny location and water regularly, keeping the soil moist but not wet.

Citrus Plants

Grapefruit, Lemons, Oranges and Limes are very easy plants to grow. Simply take the seeds from the fruit, soak them in water overnight and then plant them ¼ inch deep in potting soil. Keep the soil moist and in a week or so the seeds will spout. These houseplants have beautiful shiny leaves. Decorate a flowerpot to match the fruit and you have a wonderful gift for a friend.

This peach tree was started from seed only a year before the picture was taken. Keep in mind that apple, cherry, pear and peach seeds need a chilling period of about 60 days before they will sprout.

Aloha Pineapple Plant

The next time you purchase a pineapple, save the top. With only a few easy steps you can grow your own pineapple house plant.

1. At the local grocery store, purchase a healthy pineapple that has nice, firm, green leaves.

Materials:

Pineapple
Knife
Flower Pot
Rich Potting Soil

2. Holding onto the entire set of leaves, twist hard until the leaves come out with some stalk attached. You can also cut off the leaves and then remove any fruit so the pineapple doesn't rot.

3. Peel off the bottom layers of leaves until some small roots are exposed. Do not cut these off.

4. Place the pineapple top in a flower pot that has good drainage and add potting soil. Water regularly and fertilize monthly.

How to Grow Pineapple Fruit

If you are looking for a challenge, your family can try to force your pineapple plant to set on fruit after your pineapple plant is two years old. Put your established pineapple plant into a plastic bag. Add a couple of ripe apples to the bag and allow them rot for two weeks. The rotting apples will produce ethylene gas that will induce flowering in the pineapple. If you are lucky, after several months your pineapple plant will form a flower spike from it's center, which will eventually form a pineapple. When the pineapple fruit it about six months old, it will begin to ripen.

A good gardener always plants 3 seeds,
one for the bugs, one for the weather and one for himself.

Leo Aikman

chapter 5

Gifts from the Garden

Cotton Boll Angel

Materials:

Cotton Boll
1—One Inch Wood Ball Knob
2 Gold or White Leaves
Doll Hair
Angel Halo
Hot Glue Gun
Permanent Marker
or Paint

If growing your own cotton was not a reward in itself, then this cute project definitely will be! When finished, your angel can be used as a Christmas tree ornament or as a special gift for parents, grandparents, friends or teachers. If you want to hang the angel on the tree, hot glue a ring of ribbon onto the back of the angel.

1. Choose a cotton boll that has an "angelic" look. Remove any leaves and dirt from the cotton.

2. Cut the stem on the cotton boll down to ¼ inch. Put some hot glue into the hole on the bottom of the wood knob. Place the knob on the remaining stem. Allow to dry.

3. Place some hot glue on the back of the angel's head. Attach both leaves for wings.

4. Place a small dot of hot glue on top of the angel's head and attach the hair and halo.

5. Add the angel's facial features with a permanent marker or paint.

Hand Painted Gloves

What a fun gift to make for your mother, grandmother or a friend. These one-of-a-kind gardening gloves are not only fun and easy to make, but are a treasure when they are finished. Don't be surprised if the person you are giving them to doesn't want to get them dirty. To make a unique gardening gift, you can also paint a flower pot, and place inside of it the gloves, some inexpensive garden tools and homemade seed packets.

1. With a pencil, trace the desired design onto the gardening gloves. Try to avoid placing your design on the fingers or on the palm side of the glove. If the recipient uses the gloves in the garden these are the two areas that will see the most wear and tear.

My 5 year old, Ashlyn, painted this pair of gardening gloves all by herself.

2. When the design is complete, it is time to paint. Be sure to use fabric paint. Be creative and colorful as you paint the design on the gardening gloves.

3. Allow the paint to dry overnight. Your unique gardening gloves are now ready to "hit the dirt."

Materials:

Solid Color Gardening Gloves
Fabric Paint

Flower Pot Bird Bath

Materials:

Large Clay Flower Pot
Medium Clay Flower Pot
Large Clay Saucer
Clay Pot Sealant
Clay Pot Paint
Glass Gems
Liquid Nails™
All Purpose Clear Silicone Sealant

1. Seal the inside of the large clay saucer with clay pot sealant.

2. Paint the outside of each clay pot and the saucer with clay pot paint.

3. Glue glass gems to the top of the saucer. Place a bead of silicone sealant around the area to be decorated. Place the beads on the sealant and allow to dry.

4. Invert the large pot. Place Liquid Nails™ on the top of the large pot. Set the medium pot on top. Add a bead of Liquid Nails™ around the top edge of the pot and place the saucer on top.

5. Finish decorating the bottom areas of the birdbath using the silicone sealant and glass gems.

Bird Bath or Bird Feeder

This is the perfect activity for families to work on in the winter while waiting for the warmth of spring. It also makes a wonderful gift for a child to give to mom, grandma, friend or someone who loves birds. If you can't wait until spring to put it outside, purchase some bird seed to put in the saucer and spend the winter feeding the birds. Be careful to not let water freeze in the saucer during the winter.

Growing Loofah Sponges

Materials:

Garden Site
Loofah Sponge Seeds
Fence, Trellis or Support

1. Prepare the garden site for planting in the spring when the soil is warm and the threat of frost is over. Try to pick a sunny area that is close to a fence, or in an area where you can provide support for your new plants to climb. To improve germination, soak the seeds overnight and scrape the seed coat before planting.

I had never heard of growing loofah sponges in the home garden until Christmas a couple of years ago when my neighbor Tami gave us some of the sponges she had grown. What a fun experience you will have growing these sponges. It is also very enjoyable to give them to friends and family, and let them know you grew sponges just for them.

2. Loofah sponges require a long growing season. At the end of summer you will see that the most mature loofah sponges have skin that is turning yellow and brown. The skin will become almost paper-like. When this happens, pick the fruit and peel the skin to expose the loofah sponge. If needed, you can soak the fruit in water to help the peeling process. After the first frost, remove all additional fruit from the vine to keep it from rotting.

3. For a nice, white sponge, soak the sponge in a (3:1) water, bleach solution after peeling. Your homegrown loofah sponges can be used in the bath, for dishwashing, or you can make loofah sponge soap to give for gifts. Be sure to shake out the seeds from mature fruit to plant next year and to share with family and friends.

Loofah Sponge Soap

1. After harvesting mature loofah sponge fruit, peel and shake the seeds from the sponge.

2. Slice the loofah fruit into ½ inch slices. If desired, place the slices of sponge into a (3:1) solution of water and bleach. Let the sponges soak for several minutes until they are the desired whiteness. Rinse with water and allow them to dry on a clean towel.

3. Place a slice of sponge in each area of the soap mold.

Materials:

Loofah Sponge Fruit
Water/Bleach Solution
Soap Molds
Glycerin Soap Brick
Soap Fragrance (Optional)
Dried Flowers (Optional)

4. Melt the soap by following the manufacturer's instructions. Add the fragrance, and dried flowers if desired. Pour the melted soap into each mold, over the loofah sponge. If the sponge floats to the top, hold it down for a minute with a fork.

5. Allow the soap to harden for about 30 minutes and then remove from the mold.

6. Package the soaps for gift giving by adding a nice decorative bow.

Homemade Seed Packets

Soon after autumn arrives, you will surely find that your flower and vegetable plants have long since reached their peak. Most likely the flower petals are drooping and wilting, but soon you and your family will be able to start collecting seeds from these plants. Not only will this save you money next year, but it can also be a very rewarding experience for children.

1. To begin harvesting your garden seeds you must first determine if the seeds are mature. One good test is to lightly tap the flower stalk. If any seeds rattle or fall out easily, they are mature and ready to harvest. Seeds are best harvested late in the day when they are dry from dew. If it rains when you are ready to harvest your seeds, be sure to wait for several dry days before harvesting. After harvesting the seeds, place them in an open container for a few weeks to dry and ripen. After this period, store seed in labeled containers. If possible, the refrigerator is the perfect place.

Materials:

Paper
Markers or Crayons
Flower Seeds or
Vegetable Seeds

2. Once you have collected seeds from your flower and vegetable gardens and are ready to share them with family and friends, a fun project is to make personalized seed packets. A template is provided on the next page. You can also go to www.gardeningwithmommy.com and print the template from the web-site.

Seed Packet Template

Trace this template onto a sheet of paper. Cut out along the black lines. Fold along the lines that are marked and then glue Flap A and Flap B down with stick glue. After decorating and placing seeds inside, glue or tape Flap C down.

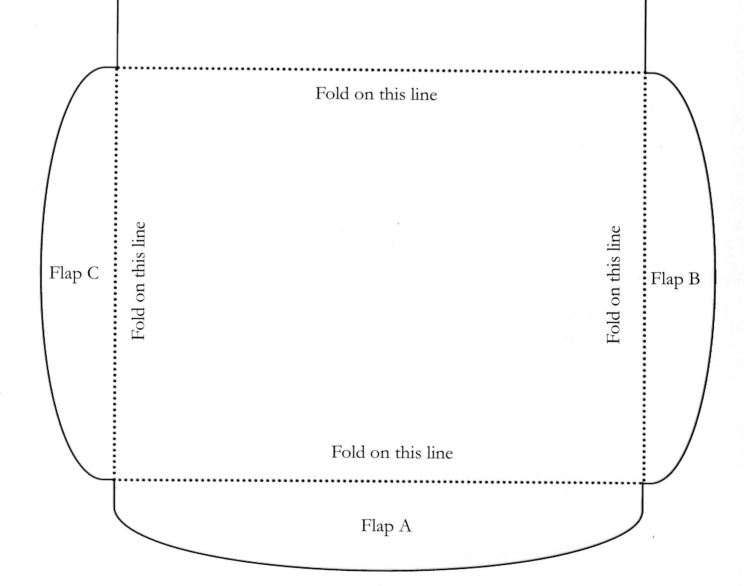

Fold on this line

Fold on this line

Fold on this line

Flap C

Fold on this line

Flap B

Fold on this line

Flap A

Pansy Painting Picture

Materials:

Pansy Flowers
Flower Petals
Mallet
White Cotton Material
Wax Paper or Clear Acetate
Printer Iron-On Transfer
  or Permanent Marker
Picture Frame

Pansies are the perfect flower to use for this project. They come in a variety of beautiful colors and the flower petals will naturally lie flat. Spring is a perfect time to harvest the flower petals, but you can do this project any time that fresh flower petals are available, either from your own garden or from plant nurseries. Be sure that the fabric is dry before you frame it behind glass. This same technique can also be used to make throw pillows or stationery.

A favorite verse can be added to the fabric with an iron-on transfer from your home computer before you start the painting process, or you can handwrite on the fabric with a fabric pen or permanent marker.

Pansy Painting Picture

1. If your fabric is wrinkled, iron it before starting this project. Arrange the flower petals face down on the white fabric until you have the desired pattern.

2. Cover the flower petals with waxed paper or clear acetate. The waxed paper and acetate will allow you to see where the petals are, and will keep the petals from sticking or moving while you hammer them.

3. Lightly tap each flower petal with the mallet. As you tap, the natural dye in the petals will stain the cotton material. When you are finished, remove the waxed paper or acetate and brush off the flower petals.

4. Once the dye has dried, the unique picture can be framed and prepared for gift giving.

The Seed is Hope;

The Flower is Joy

Plantable Seed Cards

Your family and friends will love receiving this beautiful homemade card. Even better, the paper casting attached to the front of the card will bring extra joy after it is planted and begins to grow. This project can be made any time during the year. Different paper casting molds can be used depending on the holiday, and different colors and types of cards can be purchased. Check your local craft store for all the supplies.

Materials:

Cotton Linter Sheets for Paper Making
Paper Casting Mold
Water
Blender
Small Flower Seeds
Purchased Cards or Colored Cardstock
Mesh Strainer
Small Bowl

1. Cut a piece of cotton linter the approximate size of the mold. Soak the cotton linter in one or two cups of water for 2 to 3 minutes. Blend the paper on low for 5 to 10 seconds and then on high for the same amount of time.

2. Pour the cotton linter pulp through a kitchen mesh strainer. Place the pulp in a small bowl. Add 10 to 15 flower seeds (more if desired) and mix together with the pulp.

3. Place the pulp in the casting mold, pat and press into the mold with a paper towel. Continue to press firmly with the towel until as much water as possible is removed.

4. The cotton linter can be dried using a hair dryer. Using low heat, blow air on the casting mold for several minutes until the edges start to lift from the mold. Carefully remove the cotton linter from the mold and allow to air dry overnight.

5. Make or purchase blank cards to attach the seed casting. I found beautiful handmade cards at our local craft store. Print your message on the front of the card with a permanent marker or a computer. Attach the seed casting to the card using a small amount of hot glue. Include inside the card the planting information about the seeds used in the casting.

I once planted a garden with seeds,

But as it grew Mom made me pull out all the weeds.

So next year I decided to grow seeds,

But the same thing happened again!

Alan Joyal, Age 9

Chapter 6

Holiday Gardening

Seed Packet Flower Arrangement

By the time Valentine's Day rolls around each year, our family is ready for spring to arrive so we can get back outside to enjoy our outdoor activities. This flower arrangement is fun to make, inexpensive and will delight the recipient. Whether for grandma, mom, or a favorite teacher, it makes a thoughtful gift.

"The Love of Gardening is a Seed That Once Sown Never Dies."
Gertrude Jekyll

Materials:

Decorative Vase
Floral Foam
Seed Packets
Floral Card Holders
Dried Baby's Breath
Hot Glue

1. Place floral foam in the bottom of the vase. If needed, use hot glue to hold the foam in place.

2. The floral card holders can be purchased from any flower shop. Arrange these in the floral foam. Cut the holders that will be in the front shorter to create different heights.

3. Place the seed packets in the card holders.

4. Place sprigs of baby's breath throughout the arrangement, eliminating any bare spots.

5. If desired, you can add other items, like heart picks, bows or even dried flowers to the arrangement.

Easter Egg Planter

Materials:

Eggs
Food Coloring
Vinegar
Water
Potting Soil
Seeds

Omelets anyone? You can prepare breakfast for your family and then use the empty egg shells to start plants indoors. This is a fun activity to do before Easter. Place the eggs in a basket for a beautiful display.

1. With the help of an adult, carefully cut off the top of an uncooked egg, and empty the egg into a bowl.

2. Carefully wash the shell in soap and water. Make egg dye using food coloring, vinegar and water. Color each egg and allow it to dry.

3. Fill each egg with potting soil. Plant a couple of fast growing seeds in each egg. Water each egg and wait for the seeds to sprout. After the plants sprout, place the eggs in a bright sunny window.

4. Once the plants are established they can be transplanted from their egg planters into the garden. Carefully crack the shell, remove the plant and transplant it.

"Each little flower that opens,
Each little bird that sings,
God made their glowing colors,
He made their tiny wings."

Cecil F. Alexander

Bunny Carrot Garden

Why not grow some cute, round ball-shaped carrots for your favorite bunny. This new carrot variety is perfect for containers and very easy to grow. Your container can be decorated to look like a bunny.

1. Cut out two ears from the white Funny Foam™. Cut out two smaller ears from the pink Funny Foam™. Glue the pink ears in the middle of the larger white ears.

2. With adult supervision, attach each ear to the flower pot using a hot glue gun.

3. Attach the small pom pom nose, the larger pom pom tail, the wiggly eyes, and the chenille whiskers using the hot glue gun.

4. Draw on the mouth of the bunny with a permanent marker.

5. To grow the carrot seeds, fill the flower pot with a good quality potting soil. Place the small seeds on the soil and cover with a small amount of soil. Gently water the seeds, cover with plastic wrap. In a week the seeds will sprout, remove the plastic wrap and place the flower pot in a bright sunny location and water regularly.

Materials:

White Flower Pot
White Funny Foam™
Pink Funny Foam™
Hot Glue Gun
Large Wiggle Eyes

Small Pom Pom (nose)
Large Pom Pom (tail)
Permanent Marker
Chenille Wire (Whiskers)
Thumbelina Carrot Seeds

Easter Grass Basket

Materials:

Easter Basket
Plastic to line basket
Stapler
Potting Soil
Grass Seed
Water

Fast sprouting grass seed will change an ordinary Easter basket into a growing planter. Add a few Easter eggs and you will have a fun, festive centerpiece for your table. If you want your basket to be just perfect for Easter, plan to plant the grass seed a couple of weeks before.

1. Find the perfect Easter basket to create your living Easter basket. We purchased the one shown at a local discount store for only a dollar.

2. Line the basket with plastic. A plastic trash bag can be cut down to fit inside. Staple the plastic in 6 to 8 places around the top to hold it in place. Fill the basket with potting soil.

3. Sprinkle a small handful of grass seed on top of the potting soil. With your fingers, gently mix the seeds into the top layer of soil. Gently water and cover with plastic wrap until the seeds sprout. After the grass is several inches tall, add Easter eggs for a beautiful centerpiece.

"May Day" Basket

Materials:

**Construction Paper or
  Cardstock
Glue or Stapler
Hole Punch
Ribbon
Stickers or
  Pretty Flower Pictures
Fresh Flowers**

May Baskets are fun to make for friends, family, teachers or neighbors. Prepare baskets ahead of time. Fill them with flowers and treats on May 1, hang them on the door, ring the door bell or knock and then hide. This old tradition is one that our new generation of children will absolutely love.

4. Decorate the cone with stickers, or glue on flower pictures. Add fresh flowers just before it is time to deliver this special treat.

1. Cut a square from the construction paper or cardstock. Cut off one corner as shown.

3. Punch one hole on each side of the top of the cone. Thread the ribbon through the holes and tie a bow at the top.

***April Showers
Bring
May Flowers***

2. Overlap the edges of the square to form a cone shape and glue or staple. The cut-off corner of the square will make the point of the cone.

Gardening Note:

If you are not lucky enough to have fresh garden flowers to add to your "May Basket," visit your local florist or grocery store and pick up an inexpensive bouquet. One bouquet will most likely be enough to make several baskets.

Best "MuM" in the World

Materials:

Clay Flower Pot
Paints
Chrysanthemum Plant
Potting Soil

This one-of-a-kind, hand decorated flower pot will make a wonderful Mother's Day gift that every "Mum" will enjoy. You may even want to make one for that special "Grand Mum!"

3. When the paint is dry, add potting soil and plant a beautiful blooming chrysanthemum plant. Add a bow and a handmade card, and you will have a gift for your mom that she will always treasure.

1. Using clay pot paint, paint a solid color base coat on the pot.

2. Paint the words "Best Mum" or "Best Grand Mum" on the clay pot. Decorate the pot with painted flowers, or whatever you enjoy painting.

Mother's Day
Gift Idea

Pumpkin Planter

Materials:

Carvable Imitation Pumpkin
Black Permanent Marker
Potting Soil
Grass or Wheat Seed

1. With adult supervision, cut the top off the a carvable pumpkin.

2. Using a permanent marker or paint, draw and color in the face for the pumpkin.

3. Fill the pumpkin within one to two inches of the top with potting soil.

4. Sprinkle the soil with grass or wheat seed. Sprinkle with water and wait for your pumpkin's hair to grow.

Tin Can Pumpkin Man

Materials:

Empty Vegetable Can
Orange Paint
Black Paint
White Paint
Sponge (Optional)
Potting Soil
Grass or Wheat Seed

There are so many fun pumpkin planters to do around Halloween. This one is very inexpensive because you use a vegetable can that you would normally throw away or recycle. Save a number of cans if you have a group of children doing this project.

1. Open and eat your favorite can of vegetables. Clean the can with soap and water and carefully hand dry.

2. Paint the can with a coat of orange paint. Using a sponge, apply a final coat of paint for an unusual texture.

3. After the orange paint is dry, sketch the face on the pumpkin with a pencil. Paint the facial features with black and white paint. Allow to dry.

4. Fill the can, within one inch of the top, with potting soil. Sprinkle grass or wheat seed on top of the soil. Cover with soil, gently water and then cover with plastic wrap until the seeds sprout.

Scary Haircutting Fun

1. Find a cup or decorative container that looks like it needs some hair. The Halloween cups we used were found at a dollar discount store for only one dollar.

2. Fill with potting soil and then sprinkle with wheat seed. Be generous with the seed so your creature has a lot of hair. Water and wait for the hair to start to grow.

3. Allow the hair to grow for about a week. By this time the hair should be 5 to 6 inches tall. With adult supervision, it is time to practice your hair cutting skills. Continue to water and before long it will be time to give your little guy another haircut.

Materials:

Decorative Container that has a Face
Potting Soil
Wheat Seed
Scissors

This is especially fun for small children. With some guidance, preschool-age children will be able to do this project with very little help. The grass seed sprouts very quickly, which is great for their short attention span.

Pine Cone Christmas Tree

Materials:

Pinecone
Small Flower Pot
Sand
Potting Soil
Grass Seed
Cup
Water

1. In the fall take a trip outside to hunt for pinecones. Above, Ashlyn finds pinecones just down the road from our house.

2. Prepare the flower pot by filling it within an inch of the top with sand or gravel. This will add weight to the pot and keep from wasting potting soil.

3. Cover the sand or gravel with a layer of potting soil. The potting soil will make the flower pot look like it is full of soil.

4. Soak the pinecone in a cup of water for approximately ten minutes.

5. Dip or sprinkle the pinecone with grass seed. Gently push the pinecone into the soil so that it is stable and won't fall over.

6. Cover with a plastic bag until the seeds sprout. Mist daily.

Christmas is for the Birds

1. With adult supervision string popcorn and cranberries onto clear fishing line with a needle.

2. Spread peanut butter on the pinecones and dip each pinecone into a bowl of birdseed.

Materials:

Miniature Christmas Tree
Cranberries
Popcorn
Fishing Line
Sewing Needle
Pinecones
Peanut Butter
Bird Seed
Ornamental Peppers

3. String the cranberries and popcorn on the tree and add the pinecones.

4. Add other natural decorations such as ornamental peppers and flowers. Watch as the birds enjoy their treats throughout the year. Add more decorations as old ones disappear.

This gift is not just for the birds. You entire family will find tremendous enjoyment in preparing the ornaments for the tree, and then watching as the birds come to feast from the tree all winter long. Kids will love looking around the yard to find natural items to place on the tree.

Living Christmas Ornament

Materials:

Glass Ornament
Water
Sprout Seeds
String or Ribbon

1. Remove the top of the glass ornament.

2. Pour ½ teaspoon of sprout seeds into the ornament.

3. Cover the seeds with water. Within a few days the seeds will sprout. Add additional water if needed.

Embellish your family Christmas tree with these ornaments that will grow and change daily. Keep in mind that the ornaments will most likely not be usable again. Add potting soil and seeds for another way to grow seeds inside an ornament.

One day I met a flower,
Her name was Marigold.

I was shocked by her beauty,
And her fragrant smell so bold.

So I stopped and I asked her,
If she'd like to come home with me.

"Well no", she boldly stated,
I don't think that you see.

I have many friends
all around me here,

From the birds to the bees,
To an occasional deer,

We are all a huge family,
In this garden so vast.

So continue to enjoy us,
As long as we last.

chapter 7

Gardening
Resources

Garden Language for Kids

WEED - Something that grows in your garden and you don't like it or want it there.

SOIL - The top layer of the earth's surface in which plants grow.

DIRT - Soil

ANNUAL - A plant that lives and grows through one growing season.

PERENNIAL - A plant that keeps coming back and growing, season after season.

ROOT - The part of the plant that grows usually underground, anchors the plant and supplies the plant with nourishment.

SEED - Plants produce these when mature. Each seed contains everything needed to start a new plant. They come in many different sizes and shapes.

FLOWER - Where the seeds are produced in a plant.

FLOWER BED - An area where you grow flowers.

POTTING SOIL - A mixture of soil, fertilizer, sand and peat used in pots for growing plants.

FERTILIZER - Food for plants.

SEED COAT - The outside protective covering of a seed.

SHADE - An area in the garden that receives no direct sunlight, usually in an area that has a shadow caused by a big object like a house or tree.

PARTIAL SHADE - An area that receives 1 to 5 hours of sunlight.

PARTIAL SUN - An area that receives 3 to 5 hours of full-sun everyday.

SUN - An area that receives 6 or more hours of full-sun everyday.

COMPOST - Decayed grass, leaves, plants and other organic material. Great to mix into the soil in flower beds and gardens.

Monthly Precipitation Graph

Precipitation (rain, snow, sleet or hail) is very important to gardeners. Without adequate water, plants are not able to survive. Vegetable plants rely on water not only for their own survival, but also for the production of the fruit. Water makes up to 80 to 90% of their weight when picked off the vine.

To determine the amount of rainfall for your area for a given month, watch your local weather station or do a search on the internet.

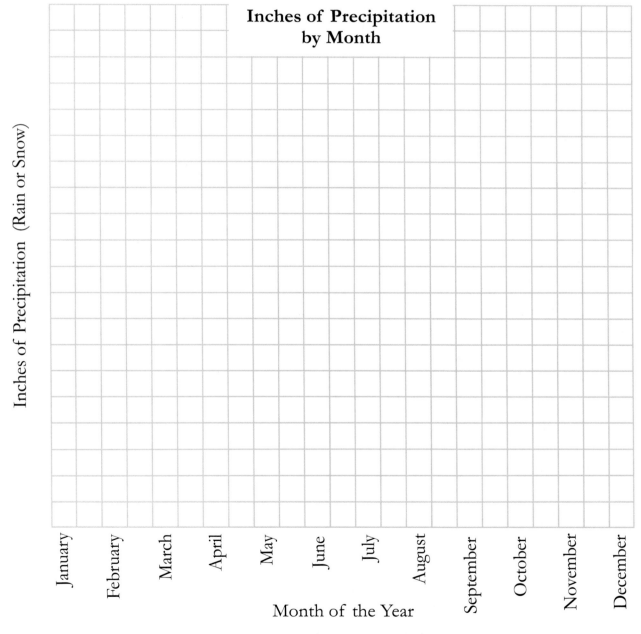

Inches of Precipitation by Month

Inches of Precipitation (Rain or Snow)

January   February   March   April   May   June   July   August   September   October   November   December

Month of the Year

Garden Design

Before planting a vegetable or flower garden, it is wise to sketch the garden on paper. Use the graph below to help with your sketch. First measure and draw in the area where the garden will be planted using a scale that 1 square equals 1 square foot in your garden.

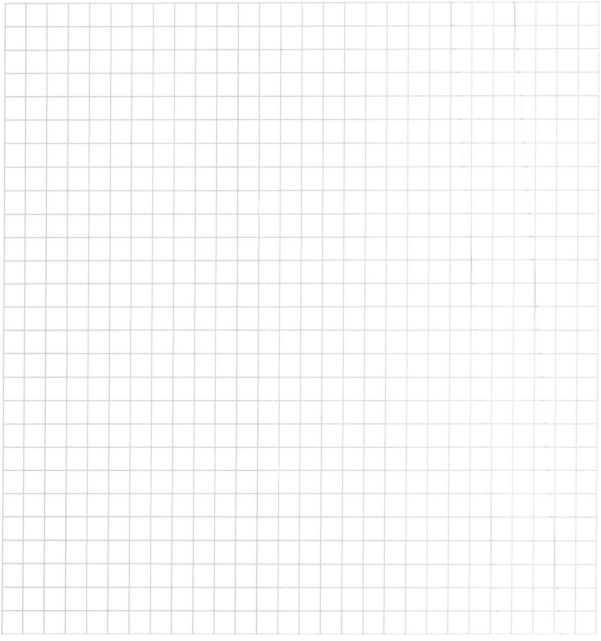

Go to www.gardeningwithmommy.com to print out more garden graphs.

Garden Design

Before planting a vegetable or flower garden, it is wise to sketch the garden on paper. Use the graph below to help with your sketch. First measure and draw in the area where the garden will be planted using a scale that 1 square equals 1 square foot in your garden.

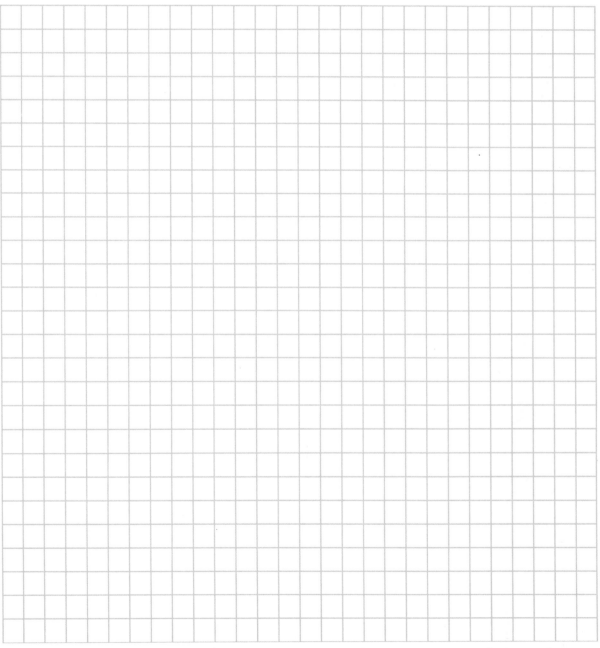

Go to www.gardeningwithmommy.com to print out more garden graphs.

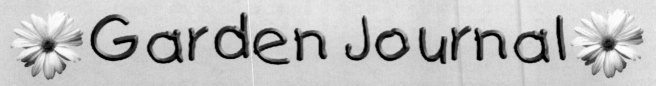

Garden Journal

Growing Flowers & Vegetables From Seed

Plant Name: _____

I planted my seeds on _____.
Date Planted

The seed packet says it will take _____ days for my seeds to sprout.
Number of Days

I think that it will take about _____ days to sprout.
Number of Days

My seeds started to sprout after _____ days.
Number of Days

I water my plant every _____ days.
Number of Days

The plant grew very _____.
Fast or Slow

The _____ really liked my plant.
Type of Insect

The plant first bloomed on _____.
Date

The first harvest came on _____.
Date

Go to www.gardeningwithmommy.com to print out more journal pages.

Garden Journal

Flowers and Vegetables Plant Information

Plant Name: _____

I planted the plant on _____.
Date Planted

The plant prefers a location that is_____.
Sunny, Shady or Part-Shade

I thought the best place to plant it would be _____.
Where the plant was planted

The plant should grow to be _____ inches high and _____ wide.

I water my plant every _____ days.
Number of Days

The plant grew very _____.
Fast or Slow

The _____ really liked my plant.
Type of Insect

The plant first bloomed on _____.
Date

The first harvest came on _____.
Date

I would definitely _____ this type of plant again.
Plant or Not Plant

Go to www.gardeningwithmommy.com to print out more journal pages.

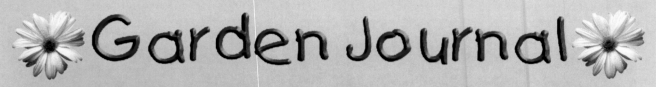

Garden Journal

Growing Flowers & Vegetables From Seed

Plant Name: _____

I planted my seeds on _____.
Date Planted

The seed packet says it will take _____ days for my seeds to sprout.
Number of Days

I think that it will take about _____ days to sprout.
Number of Days

My seeds started to sprout after _____ days.
Number of Days

I water my plant every _____ days.
Number of Days

The plant grew very _____.
Fast or Slow

The _____ really liked my plant.
Type of Insect

The plant first bloomed on _____.
Date

The first harvest came on _____.
Date

Go to www.gardeningwithmommy.com to print out more journal pages.

Garden Journal

Flowers and Vegetables Plant Information

Plant Name: _____

I planted the plant on _____.
Date Planted

The plant prefers a location that is_____.
Sunny, Shady or Part-Shade

I thought the best place to plant it would be _____.
Where the plant was planted

The plant should grow to be _____ inches high and _____ wide.

I water my plant every _____ days.
Number of Days

The plant grew very _____.
Fast or Slow

The _____ really liked my plant.
Type of Insect

The plant first bloomed on _____.
Date

The first harvest came on _____.
Date

I would definitely _____ this type of plant again.
Plant or Not Plant

Go to www.gardeningwithmommy.com to print out more journal pages.

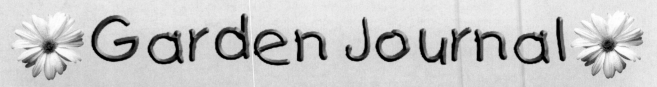

Garden Journal

Growing Flowers & Vegetables From Seed

Plant Name: _____

I planted my seeds on _____.
  Date Planted

The seed packet says it will take _____ days for my seeds to sprout.
  Number of Days

I think that it will take about _____ days to sprout.
  Number of Days

My seeds started to sprout after _____ days.
  Number of Days

I water my plant every _____ days.
  Number of Days

The plant grew very _____.
  Fast or Slow

The _____ really liked my plant.
  Type of Insect

The plant first bloomed on _____.
  Date

The first harvest came on _____.
  Date

Go to www.gardeningwithmommy.com to print out more journal pages.

Garden Journal

Flowers and Vegetables Plant Information

Plant Name: _____

I planted the plant on _____.
Date Planted

The plant prefers a location that is_____.
Sunny, Shady or Part-Shade

I thought the best place to plant it would be _____.
Where the plant was planted

The plant should grow to be _____ inches high and _____ wide.

I water my plant every _____ days.
Number of Days

The plant grew very _____.
Fast or Slow

The _____ really liked my plant.
Type of Insect

The plant first bloomed on _____.
Date

The first harvest came on _____.
Date

I would definitely _____ this type of plant again.
Plant or Not Plant

Go to www.gardeningwithmommy.com to print out more journal pages.

Seasonal Gardening Guide

Spring: Summer:

Wizard of Oz Garden
Pizzeria Garden
"Wild Animal" Zoo Garden
Herb Garden
Spaghetti Sauce Garden
Chocolate Garden
Grow an Apple & a Swan
Rainbow Garden
The Itsy Bitsy Spider Garden
Outer Space Garden
Hawaiian Aloha Garden
ABC Garden
Gardening Rocks Garden
Candy Garden
Salad Container Garden
Colander Herb Garden
Cotton Garden
Tree Blossom Bouquet
Pansy Painting Picture
Easter Egg Planter
Bunny Carrot Garden
Easter Grass Basket
"May Day" Basket
Best "Mum" in the World
Growing Loofah Sponges
Fun Plants to Grow

Winter:

Seed Packet Flower Arrangement
Pine Cone Christmas Tree
Living Christmas Ornament
Christmas is for the Birds
Cotton Boll Angel

Fall:

Loofah Sponge Soap
Pansy Painting Picture
Salad Container Garden
Pumpkin Planter
Tin Can Pumpkin Man
Scary Haircutting Fun

Anytime:

Grass Sock Caterpillar
Goldfish Plant Garden
Crystal Rock Garden
Fun Plant Planters
Rainbow Bouquet
Layered Soil Dessert
Grocery Store Gardening
Aloha Pineapple Plant
Hand Painted Gardening Gloves
Flower Pot Bird Bath
Homemade Seed Packets
Plantable Seed Cards
Cactus Boot Garden
Litter Box Garden

Acknowledgements

I would like to offer thanks to all the following people that worked so hard to make this book a reality.

To my husband Roger. Without your support, patience, expertise and love, this book never would have been possible. Thank you for always believing in me. May we have a lifetime of projects and gardens to work on together.

To Alan and Ashlyn, thank you for helping me grow so many gardens and work on so many activities. I hope that the time we have spent together means as much to you as it does to me.

To my parents, thank you for introducing me to gardening, for showing me the joy that can be found in digging in the soil and for your love and support.

To Kelly Welch, for his wonderful painting of Ashlyn.

To Karen and Eldon Younce for doing such a wonderful job of editing the book.

And last but not least, to all of our family and friends for the support we received throughout the duration of this project. You have all been so supportive, were always willing to listen to my ideas and updates. I will never forget your kindness.

My thanks to each one of you,

Kristen Joyal

Baking with Mommy Cookbook:
Recipes for Kid-Size Ovens

Recipes designed for: the Easy Bake Oven(TM), Barbie(TM) Bake with Me Oven, Mrs. Fields(TM) Baking Factory and other light bulb ovens.

Dash, Pinch & Smidgen Measuring Spoon Set

Each measuring spoon is an exact measurment:
1/8 teaspoon = Dash
1/16 teaspoon = Pinch
1/32 teaspoon = Smidgen

Measuring spoons are made of high quality nylon and are dishwasher safe.

Apron

Kid-Size fabric Apron fits any youth age and are premium quality!

Available at
www.bakingwithmommy.com
or 316.207.3211
info@bakingwithmommy.com

Chef Hat

Professional cloth chef hat with a Velcro(TM) adjustment that fits any youth AND any adult!

The Joyal Family
Alan, Kristen, Roger and Ashlyn

Recipes designed for: Easy Bake Oven™, Queasy Bake™ Cookerator™, Easy Bake Real Meal Oven™, Mrs. Fields™ Baking Factory and other light bulb ovens